DOES
ATHEISM
MAKE
SENSE?

JOHN BLANCHARD

First published in Great Britain in 2006

Reprinted 2021

British Library Cataloguing in Publication Data
A record for this book is available from the British Library

ISBN: 978-1-783971-84-8

Cover design by Pete Barnsley (CreativeHoot.com)

Evangelical Press (EP Books), an imprint of 10Publishing
Unit C, Tomlinson Road, Leyland, PR25 2DY, England

www.epbooks.org
epbooks@10ofthose.com

Contents

Introduction

Atheism is the theory or belief that God does not exist. The idea has had a long shelf life, and it made dramatic progress in Russia in the first half of the twentieth century when the Communist revolutionary Vladimir Lenin became frustrated that hard-core socialism had not wiped out religion. In his opinion, 'Every religious idea, every idea of God, every flirtation with the idea of God, is unutterable vileness.' He told the Soviet author Maxim Gorky, 'There can be nothing more abominable than religion' and persuaded his fellow leaders that God should be eliminated from every area of society. They did this by decreeing that 'the teaching of school subjects (history, literature, natural sciences, physics, chemistry, etc.) should be saturated with atheism.'

From then on the anti-religion drive gathered pace and power. State-led propaganda, brainwashing, imprisonment, torture and execution were all used as the crusade spread throughout Eastern Europe, then to the Far East and elsewhere. Since then, countless people around the world have been repressed, bullied, tortured, imprisoned or killed for no other reason than that they believed in the existence of God and by 1960 it was estimated that half the population of the world was nominally atheist.

The signs were such that in 1966 TIME magazine asked on its front cover of 8 April, 'Is God dead?' However, in its 7 April 1980 issue it told its readers, 'In a quiet revolution that no one could have foreseen only two decades ago, God is making a comeback. Now it is more respectable among philosophers than it has been for a generation to talk about the possibility of God's existence.'

The *Economist* took the same line in its millennium issue and published what it called God's obituary, but towards the end of 2007 admitted that in doing so it had overstepped the mark.

The American author Paul Johnson went even further: 'The most extraordinary thing about the twentieth century was the failure of God to die. The collapse of mass religious belief, especially among the educated and prosperous, had been widely and confidently predicted. It did not take place. Somehow, God survived, flourished even. At the end of the twentieth century the idea of a personal, living God is as lively and real as ever in the minds and hearts of countless millions of men and women throughout our planet.'

At the turn of the millennium the social and political movement New Atheism came on stream, marked by the ferocious way in which it aggressively attacked religion, claiming that it was not only wrong but evil. Its leading strike force – the British biologist Richard Dawkins, one of today's most vocal atheists, the Anglo-American author Christopher Hitchens, and the American philosophers Daniel Dennett and Sam Harris – became known as The Four Horsemen, and all produced best-selling books laying heavily into religion of every kind, and especially into Christianity. In explaining his purpose in writing *The God Delusion*, Richard Dawkins says, 'I am attacking God, all

6

gods, anything and everything supernatural, wherever and whenever they have been or will be invented.' On the next page he adds: 'Unless otherwise stated, I shall have Christianity mostly in mind.'

At a 2012 'Reason Rally' in Washington, DC he told the crowd how to deal with Christians: 'Mock them, ridicule them in public...Don't fall for the convention that we're too polite to talk about religion.' In God Is Not Great, Christopher Hitchens wrote, 'Religion poisons everything'. In *Darwin's Dangerous Idea*, Daniel Dennett dismisses God as 'a myth of childhood, not anything a sane, undeluded adult could literally believe in' and says he must 'either be turned into a symbol for something less concrete or abandoned altogether.' In *Letter to a Christian Nation*, Sam Harris writes, 'Atheism is nothing more than the noises reasonable people make in the presence of unjustified religious beliefs,' and says that it was neither a philosophy nor even a view of the world, but 'simply an admission of the obvious.'   Elsewhere he claims, 'The problem is that religion... allows perfectly sane and perfectly intelligent people to believe en masse what only idiots or lunatics could believe in isolation.'

This is strong stuff and is clearly meant to be convincing – but is it? Does atheism make sense...?

1 Does atheism make cosmic sense

On 5 August 2011 NASA launched its Juno spacecraft from Cape Canaveral, Florida, with a goal to 'understand and explore the origin and evolution of Jupiter', the gas giant that is the largest planet in our solar system. On 4 July 2016 Juno reached Jupiter's orbit, and in a manoeuvre timed to within a fraction of a second, cut its speed by 1,212 miles (1,950 kilometres) per hour in order to be captured by Jupiter's gravitational pull and begin its closer examination of the planet. Although sometimes travelling at speeds in excess of 250,000 miles (402,000 kilometres) per hour, Juno had taken nearly five years to get there. Yet Jupiter is only the fifth (of eight) planets in distance from the sun in a solar system that, as the British theoretical physicist Stephen Hawking puts it, is in the 'outer suburbs' of the Milky Way galaxy, one of 100,000 million galaxies in the known universe. No wonder the English author Douglas Adams came up with what may be the best-known words in his multi-media phenomenon The Hitchhiker's Guide to the Galaxy: 'Space is big. Really big. You just won't believe how vastly mind-bogglingly big it is. I mean, you may think it's a long way down the road to the chemist, but that's just peanuts to space.'

Adams' quirky comment has had a long shelf life, but he could not have predicted the scientific discoveries which would be made within a few decades and which would open up the vast reaches of the universe as never before. In 2016, world-ranking physicists announced that they had made what was hailed as the scientific breakthrough of the century, one that would revolutionize all future astronomy. Ninety-nine years earlier, the German physicist Albert Einstein claimed that space-time was not a void but a four-dimensional 'fabric' that could change shape as gravitational waves moved through it, though he could not prove this. In the nineteen-seventies scientists began to develop a Laser Interferometer Gravitational-Wave Observatory (LIGO) that could test Einstein's theory.   LIGO is actually two observatories nearly 1,900 miles (3,058 kilometres) apart, one in Louisiana and one in Washington state, and when they became operational they discovered exactly what Einstein had predicted.

The LIGO team also came to the conclusion that these gravitational waves were triggered off more than a billion years ago when deep in space two massive black holes (collapsed stars so dense that not even light can escape from them) collided and merged. The impact was so violent that its power has been estimated at fifty times greater than the combined power of all the stars in the universe, and sent ripples (gravitational waves) out in all directions.   Laser physicist David Reitze, who had first suggested building LIGO, said, 'It's mind boggling. It's the first time the universe has spoken to us through gravitational waves. Until now we have been deaf to gravitational waves, but now we can hear... I think we're opening a window to the universe.'

Several illustrations have been used to explain the effect of a massive black hole collision. A heavy ball placed on a taut rubber sheet causes the sheet to sag. If a smaller ball is then placed near the first one, gravity will cause it to fall towards the larger one, and the sheet will bend and ripple. As gravity in deep space is much stronger than it is on earth, the collision of two black holes is unimaginably violent, space itself is bent and stretched, and vast ripples are generated. Dragging a hand through a still pool of water, or dropping a stone into it are other simple ways of creating ripples and giving us at least an inkling of what happens when black holes collide.

As well as providing the first physical proof that black holes exist, LIGO's results give us a staggering illustration of the vastness of the universe. Although travelling at the speed of light (186,282 miles – or 299,792 kilometres – per second) these 'ripples' (gravitational waves) took 1.6 billion years to reach our planet. As the universe is constantly expanding we will never be able to fix on a precise size – but Douglas Adams' 'mind-bogglingly big' fits the bill. In 1997 the Royal Astronomical Society reported new data showing that the universe was then ten per cent larger than we thought. In 2016 NASA's Kepler space telescope discovered more than 1,200 new planets in our galaxy alone – and these were all in one small patch of night sky. It is not surprising that Richard Dawkins experiences 'a colossal sense of awe and wonder' whenever he thinks about the cosmos.

This all raises massive questions for the atheist and we can only touch on the most fundamental one here, famously framed like this by the eighteenth-century German mathematician and philosopher Gottfried Leibniz: 'The first question which should rightly be asked will be, why is there something rather than nothing. That is, why does anything at all exist?' The British one-time Oxford professor of chemistry Peter Atkins, a hard-line atheist, endorses what has become known as the quantum fluctuation hypothesis by suggesting that 'space-time generates its own dust in the process of its own self-assembly', an empty soundbite matching his claim that the entire universe, with all its amazing interlocking order, is 'an elaborate and engaging rearrangement of nothing'.

The American theoretical scientist physicist and cosmologist Lawrence Krauss, a passionate atheist who claims that his scientific discoveries deny the existence of God, says much the same kind of thing in his 2012 book *Universe from Nothing*. Taking up the issue of how 'something' arises from 'nothing' he writes, 'By nothing I do not mean nothing but rather nothing – in this case, the nothingness we normally call empty space.' Far from explaining anything, Krauss misses the point that 'empty space' is anything but empty. Instead, it is crammed with energy, particles and anti-particles (otherwise known as virtual particles) that are constantly flitting into and out of existence, facts that physicists have known for decades. The Oxford mathematician and philosopher John Lennox puts comments like these into perspective: 'Nonsense remains nonsense, even when talked by world-famous scientists.'

The most popular theory about the origin of the cosmos claims that millions of years ago a 'Big Bang' brought it into being, and atheists buy big-time into this idea, in spite of the fact that it raises massive questions nobody has been able to answer. If the whole universe as we now know it was nothing more than a microscopic particle, where did it come from? Why and how did it suddenly become unstable and explode without something (or someone) outside of itself acting upon it? Even if we accept such an Alice in Wonderland idea, why should this random shuffling of 'nothing' produce the elegant, precisely-tuned laws of physics that govern the present universe? The English scholar Keith Ward, a Fellow of the British Academy, shows where this kind of thinking leads: 'One day there might be nothing. The next day, there might be a very large carrot. Nothing else in existence whatsoever, all alone and larger than life, a huge carrot. If anything is possible, that certainly is. The day after that, the carrot might disappear and be replaced by a purple spotted gorilla. Why not? ... Why does this thought seem odd, or even ridiculous, whereas the thought that some law of physics might just pop into existence does not? Logically, they are exactly on a par.'

The American theoretical physicist Michio Kaku, one of the world's most respected scientists, has no religious axe to grind, yet says, 'To me it is clear that we exist in a plan which is governed by rules that were created, shaped by a universal intelligence and not by chance.' He also claims that the very purpose of physics is 'to find an equation which will allow us to unify all the forces of nature and allow us to read the mind of God.'

The Nobel Prize-winning American physicist and radio astronomer Arno Penzias has this to say on the subject: 'Astronomy leads us to a unique event, a universe that was created out of nothing and delicately balanced to provide exactly the right conditions required to support life. In the absence of an absurdly-improbable accident, the observations of modern science seem to suggest an underlying, one might say, supernatural plan.' Accepting a prestigious award for his work he added, 'the creation of the universe is supported by all the observable data astronomy has produced so far'.

For the British philosopher (and outspoken atheist) Bertrand Russell to shrug off the cosmos with, 'I should say that the universe is just there, and that's all' gets us nowhere. Science tells us that no observable effect is without a cause; so the highly ordered universe in which we live must have a cause outside of itself. Many people try to dodge the issue by suggesting the existence of a multiverse (or meta-universe), with a finite (or even infinite) number of parallel universes other than our own, but this simply kicks the can down the road, as multiple universes would need even more explanation that the existence of the one we know. What is more, how could millions of other universes rule God out? If he created one universe, surely he could create as many as he liked? Stephen Hawking's alternative is to claim that 'a great many universes were created out of nothing', and that they 'arise naturally from physical laws', but this kicks the can even further down the road, then leaves us with no explanation as to how the laws (which would have had to pre-exist nature) came into existence. Does this make sense?

2 Does atheism make reasonable sense?

In 2003 the retired American biology teacher Paul Geisert and his wife Mynga Futrell hit the headlines by using an adjective to invent a noun. The word 'bright' can mean 'shining', 'clear', 'vivid' and 'cheerful'. It can also mean 'intelligent', and the Geiserts seem to have had this definition in mind when they capitalized it and called themselves 'Brights', insisting that from then on their new word was a definitive noun. They defined a Bright as someone whose ethics and actions are based on a naturalistic worldview, free from all supernatural and spiritual elements.

Brights may not openly call themselves atheists, but they do include all who identify themselves as rationalists, humanists, secularists, naturalists, freethinkers, agnostics or sceptics. However, atheists who wear magnets to ward off disease, make decisions as a result of what they read in horoscopes, arrange their office or house furniture using feng shui, or set store by palmistry, tarot cards or other occult practices would not qualify as Brights, because they are reaching out to the supernatural world.

Geisert attended the Godless Americans March in Washington DC in 2002, but decided to look for a better term than 'godless' to identify what he called 'the community of reason'. The Brights now have an official website and thousands of members in over 200 countries. Blogs and books, events and endorsements fuel what someone has cleverly called 'The Charge of the Bright Brigade', and soundbites like these from its members give a good idea of what it stands for: 'The Brights: Removing the super from superstition'; 'Better Living through Reason'; 'Rational thinking in an irrational world'; '100% natural. No added superstition'.

The movement's name has been criticized by some who say that it suggests its members are more intelligent than those who are not; Christopher Hitchens called its title 'cringe-making'. However, Richard Dawkins had no hesitation in endorsing the idea. He told The Guardian, 'Words are not trivial. They matter because they raise consciousness... Bright? Yes, Bright is the word. I am a Bright.' When he asked elsewhere, 'Have you ever met an uneducated atheist?' it is hardly rocket science to know what he meant, and he could not have made his position clearer than when dismissing someone's religious beliefs as being 'ignominious, contemptible, retarded'. In The God Delusion he seems to hedge his bets a little by saying that he would count himself as being among those who think God is 'very improbable', but as leaning towards those who would say, 'I know there is no God.' He fine-tunes this by adding, 'I am agnostic only to the extent that I am agnostic about fairies at the bottom of the garden.'

Many atheists would sign up to this as a recognition of the fact that it is impossible to prove the existence of God.

They might even claim that this is a reasonable position to take – but is it? The issue here is whether it is reasonable or logical to assume, let alone prove, that God does not exist. As the only honest reason for believing anything is to claim a sound basis for doing so, what is the evidence for the non-existence of God? Is there scientific evidence? Is there mathematical evidence? Is there evidence from experience?

At this point, atheism runs into even greater difficulty, because it insists that the material world is all there is, and that human beings are merely complex collections of some of its fundamental particles. The British academic, novelist and poet C. S. Lewis explained the problem with this idea: 'If the solar system was brought about by an accidental collision, then the appearance of organic life on this planet was also an accident, and the whole evolution of man was an accident too. If so, then all our present thoughts are mere accidents — the accidental by-product of the movement of atoms...why should we believe them to be true? I see no reason for believing that one accident should be able to give me a correct account of all the other accidents. It's like expecting that the accidental shape taken by the splash when you upset a milk jug should give you a correct account of how the jug was made and why it was upset.'

Atheism has no answer to this. If reasonable thinking is brought about by the random shuffling of mindless particles in the brain's billions of nerve cells, why should we trust the laws of logic, or what we claim to be reasonable thinking? The distinguished British biologist J.B.S.Haldane, described as 'perhaps the most brilliant science popularizer of his generation', was a convinced atheist, yet he could see that on this issue atheism tripped over its own feet: 'It seems to me immensely unlikely that mind is a mere by-product of matter. For if my mental processes are determined wholly by the motions of atoms in my brain I have no reason to suppose that my beliefs are true. They may be sound chemically, but that does not make them sound logically. And hence I have no reason for supposing my brain to be composed of atoms.'

I have yet to come across an atheist who can give an answer to this. Nor do I understand how anybody could intelligently claim to have found one, as they would have no reason to suppose or claim that anything they thought or said was true. As far as the reliability of human reasoning is concerned, atheism cuts off the very branch on which it sits. Is it rational to believe that our ability to reason was never intended to lead us to the truth, yet irrational to believe that it was specifically designed and created to do so? Claiming that logical thinking is a by-product of evolution is no more than a shot in the dark, nor does it hit the target, as atheism claims that evolution's big concern is not truth but (to use one of its own mantras) the survival of the fittest. As matter has no life in itself, how can it generate life that has the ability think and then, in the process of thinking to decide that matter is lifeless?

Reason is closely linked to logic, which is supremely expressed in the language of mathematics, and of which there is no sign in lifeless matter. Is it reasonable to assume that what I consider to be sensible and true can be treated as such merely because the neurons in my brain happen to be arranged in a certain way? Intelligent thinking owes its existence either to lifeless matter or to a living, intelligent and superior reality that brought it into existence. There is no wiggle room here – it must be one or the other.

Atheism asks us to believe that logic and reason have no logical or reasonable origin, that there is no creative intelligence behind the universe, that our ability to think, understand, know and decide are unintended consequences of something or other, that our longing for meaning and purpose has no built-in basis, that our sense of true and false is accidental and that nothing which seems to be intricately designed has a designer. Is that position very bright?

3 Does atheism make scientific sense?

Countless people have taken on board the idea that there is a war going on between science and God-centred religion, and that it is a very one-sided battle, with science the all-conquering hero and God falling flat on his face whenever they contest an issue.

Richard Dawkins tells us, 'I think science really has fulfilled the need that religion did in the past, of explaining things, explaining why we are here, what is the origin of life, where did the world come from, what life is all about.... science has the answers.' Not to be outdone, Peter Atkins made this claim in the course of an Oxford debate: 'I am on the brink of discovering everything and I commend you to use your brains, because your brains are the most wonderful instruments in the universe — and through your brains you will see that you can do without God. There is no necessity for God, because science can explain everything.' Elsewhere, while accepting that science 'emerged from religion' he used an illustration from nature and said that it has now 'discarded its chrysalis and taken over the heath,' with the result that 'there is no reason to suppose that science cannot deal with every aspect of existence'. The American theoretical physicist Steven Weinberg adds that as far as he is concerned, 'The world needs to wake up from the long nightmare of religion... anything we scientists can do to weaken the hold of religion should be done, and may in fact be our greatest contribution to civilisation.'

If these statements are true, science alone can tell us everything we need to know about life (or anything else) and trying to make a case for belief in God is pointless - but before accepting this there are several important things we need to take on board. The first is perfectly obvious: *statements by scientists are not necessarily scientific statements.* An opinion is not the same as a fact, and we could hardly expect card-carrying atheists to allow God even a foothold in the door of their scientific assumptions. The all-important thing to establish about the statements in the last paragraph is not whether they are sincerely held by reputable scientists, but whether they are true.

The second thing to note is that science is not an end in itself, but a means to an end. It is a process, not a finished product. In true science, the latest word must never be taken as the last word. The Austrian-British thinker Sir Karl Popper, generally regarded as one of the 20th Century's greatest philosophers of science, put this well when he said, 'Every scientific statement must remain tentative for ever.' The distinguished American theoretical physicist Richard Feynman went even further: 'Scientific knowledge is a body of statements of varying degrees of certainty – some unsure, some nearly sure, but none absolutely certain.'

Thirdly, there are hugely important issues on which science is silent, and it is easy to list examples. It is unable to explain how or why the universe came into being or why it is governed by consistent and dependable laws. As we will see later on in this book, it is unable to lay down moral principles – or explain those that already exist; Richard Dawkins admits, 'Science has no method for deciding what is ethical.' It is unable to tell us whether human life has any meaning or purpose. The brilliant British biologist Sir Peter Medawar widened the picture: 'The existence of a limit to science...is made clear by its inability to answer childlike elementary questions having to do with first and last things – questions such as: "How did everything begin?"; "What are we all here for?"; "What is the point of living?"'

Fourthly, far from being able to assure us that God does not exist, science can have nothing to say on the subject, as it is outside of its range. The American evolutionary biologist Stephen Jay Gould admitted that science 'simply cannot (by its legitimate methods) adjudicate the issue of God's possible existence. We neither affirm it nor deny it; we simply can't comment on it as scientists.' Science is the ongoing process of discovering truth in the natural world – and as God is not part of the natural world he is beyond the reach of science. As the American geneticist Francis Collins, best-known for his leadership of the Human Genome Project, puts it, 'If God exists, then he must be outside the natural world, and therefore the tools of science are not the right ones to learn about him.' This is not to downgrade science in any way, but it can no more adjudicate on the question of the existence of God than a state-of-the-art peashooter can launch a moon rocket.

When Peter Atkins claims that 'science can explain everything' he is tripping over his own feet, as science is unable even to explain itself, or to tell us why we should trust it without question or qualification. In making his absurd claim Atkins is sliding from science into *scientism*, a different thing altogether. Scientism puts science on a pedestal and says with Bertrand Russell, 'What science cannot discover, mankind cannot know.' Scientism is also known as 'reductionism', but the Scottish scientist Donald MacKay invented an even better word to describe it. He called it 'nothing-buttery', as scientism says that there is nothing but matter and events caused by matter. In effect, this means that 'What you see is what you get' – but how do we know this? When scientism claims that only what can be known by science is true it is imploding, as the claim is in itself not one that can be proved scientifically. The American nuclear scientist Ian Hutchinson illustrates its fatal flaw: 'To claim there is nothing knowable outside the scope of science would be similar to a successful fisherman saying that whatever he can't catch in his nets does not exist. Once you accept that science is the only source of human knowledge, you have adopted a philosophical position (scientism) that cannot be verified, or falsified, by science itself.' In other words, scientism is by definition unscientific. It is running on fumes.

Then what about those who believe that there is a war between true science (not scientism) and religion of any kind – and then claim that it is a hopeless mismatch, with science the outright winner? In the Oxford debate mentioned earlier Peter Atkins called religion 'outmoded and ridiculous' and claimed that it was 'not possible to believe in gods and be a true scientist', while elsewhere he went for the jugular and called God 'this incompetent figment of impoverished imaginations.' This leaves us in no doubt about how he views the 'war', but neither history nor common sense are on his side.

Although the word 'scientist' was not used until 1834, science goes back much further than we can trace – the earliest scientists were those who first asked questions about why things exist – but we can pick up clear signs in the records we have of Greek philosophers nearly 3,000 years ago. We have no space to quote these thinkers here, but we can pick up the trail in the 16th Century. What stands out as we trace this is that most of its pioneers rejected scientism out of hand, as they did the pagan idea that the universe contained the answer for its own existence. Instead, they were increasingly convinced that the universe's amazing intricacy and order had only one explanation: it was brought into existence by an intelligent and powerful Creator. This is confirmed by the fact that in 1662 the founders of The Royal Society, Britain's oldest and most prestigious scientific body of its kind, dedicated their work 'to the glory of God'. As John Lennox puts it, 'Far from belief in God hindering science, it is the motor that drove it.'

To give details of ground-breaking scientists from then on who saw (and those who still see) no conflict between science and belief in God, would make this a very long book. The list would include the British philosopher Francis Bacon, who launched the inductive method in science; the German astronomer Johannes Kepler, the founder of modern astronomy; the French genius Blaise Pascal; the Irish physician Robert Boyle, sometimes called the father of modern chemistry; the Danish scientist Niels Steno, the founder of modern geology; the English mathematician and physicist Isaac Newton, who formulated the three laws of motion; the Swedish Carolus Linnaeus, known as the father of modern taxonomy; the British chemist and physicist Michael Faraday who discovered electromagnetic induction;

the British physicist James Joule, who gave his name to Joule's laws, the first about heat produced by an electric current and the second about how the energy of a gas relates to pressure, volume and temperature; the British physicist William Thomson (Baron Kelvin), who established what is now known as the Kelvin scale of absolute temperatures and gave precise terminology to the First and Second Laws of Thermodynamics; and the British scientist James Clerk Maxwell, who has been called 'the father of modern physics'.

These are just a few examples of the many that could be given, and they are followed by huge numbers of brilliant contemporary scientists, including Nobel Prize winners, who see no conflict between science and belief in God. This does not of course prove God's existence, but it shows why Stephen Jay Gould could say, 'Unless at least half my colleagues are dunces, there can be ... no conflict between science and religion.' Writing in *The Spectator*, the British journalist Melanie Phillips drew her readers' attention to the fact that 'contrary to popular myth' Western science was based on the claim that 'the universe was the product of a rational Creator, who endowed man with reason so that he could ask questions about the natural world'.

The American psychologist Paul Bloom says that 'religion and science will always clash', and Peter Atkins claims that science is 'progressively advancing towards complete knowledge, leaving religions bobbing about in its wake'.   In the light of what we have seen in this section does it make sense to agree with either of these comments?

4 Does atheism make living sense?

For as far back as we have been able to trace, man has wondered whether earth is the only planet in the universe on which life is to be found. The Greek philosopher Anaximander, who died around 546 BC, opened the door to the idea that there might be an infinite universe, and from then on men began to ask whether there could be life in other parts of it. In the sixteenth century the Italian monk and astrologer Giordano Bruno promoted the idea that an infinite universe was filled with planets that supported life, but the Roman Inquisition was so offended by this and other ideas he had that in 1600 he was burned upside down and naked in Rome's Campo de'Fiori.

Nobody since then seems to have suffered Bruno's fate for holding similar ideas, but the subject has continued to fascinate man. In 1960 the American astronomer Frank Drake launched SETI (The Search for Extraterrestrial Intelligence) and said that the project was really a search for ourselves - who we are and where we fit into the cosmic scheme of things. In the same decade the American astrophysicist Carl Sagan went so far as to suggest, 'The search for life elsewhere is something that runs so deep in human curiosity that there is not a human being anywhere in the world who isn't interested in that question.' When in 2016 it was announced that China was to demolish the homes of 9,000 people to make room for the world's largest radio telescope, an editorial in *South China Morning Post* announced, 'Our eyes and ears are closing in on the possibility of life on another planet.'

The study of life elsewhere in the universe is known as exobiology, and has been called one of the few disciplines that functions in the absence of any first-hand data. The popularity of science fiction films reflects our fascination with the possibility of life on other planets. In 1982 Hollywood gave us *E.T. the Extra-Terrestrial*, the story of an alien left behind on earth when his family returned home. *The X-files* became the longest running science fiction series in U.S. television history (1993-2002) and spawned two films. The series, with its investigation into alien abduction, was revived in 2016. *Avatar*, the 2009 American epic science-fiction film, became the highest grossing film of all time. In it humans are colonising Pandora, a moon in the Alpha Centauri system. Alleged sightings of Unidentified Flying Objects (UFOs) add to the speculation that we are not alone in the universe, but in spite of unmanned space exploration projects costing billions of pounds nobody has yet found any concrete evidence of life anywhere else but on our comparatively small planet, which Stephen Hawking neatly called 'a medium-sized planet orbiting around an average star in the outer suburbs of an ordinary spiral galaxy, which is itself only one of about a million million galaxies in the observable universe'. Carl Sagan was inspired and humbled by an image of earth taken by a spacecraft from a record distance of 3.7 billion miles, describing it as 'a lonely speck in the great enveloping cosmic darkness', and reflecting that 'every saint and every sinner in the history of our species has lived there, on a mote of dust suspended in a sunbeam.'

Yet on that 'mote of dust' there are said to be about 8.7 million living species, 6.5 million on land and 2.2 million in its oceans. The vast majority of them have not yet been identified, and it has been estimated that cataloguing them would take 1,000 years. Why is there such a staggering difference between our little planet and the rest of the universe? What makes it so special? Some believe life on our planet is the result of either accidental panspermia (micro-organisms falling to earth from meteorites) or directed panspermia (intelligent aliens deliberately dumping spores here by means of a manned or unmanned spacecraft). Yet in the total absence of any evidence these ideas can be filed under 'Science Fiction', and in any case trying to explain life on our planet in this way merely sweeps the problem of life's origin under some other corner of the cosmic carpet.

Although stars and planets account for only about one per cent of the universe's mass (or matter) it would need to be extraordinarily fine-tuned for life to exist and thrive anywhere in it. This fine-tuning involves the relationship between four fundamental forces of nature – gravity, electromagnetism, the strong nuclear force and the weak nuclear force. I have written about this elsewhere and can only touch on it here. To give one example, if gravity were even slightly stronger or weaker, planets could not exist, yet the forces of gravity and electromagnetism are perfectly balanced to allow this. The American cosmologist Edward Kolb says, 'The universe, it seems, is fine-tuned to let life and consciousness flower.' The strong and weak nuclear forces are also balanced with amazing precision, allowing protons, neutrons and electrons to form atoms. If protons were not exactly 1,836 more massive than electrons, intelligent life could not be maintained or developed.

There is room here to mention only one other 'coincidence'. It relates to the conditions necessary for the formation of carbon and oxygen, the two elements essential for life. Here, the precise energy levels involved are so meticulous that two British authors, the Astronomer Royal Sir Martin Rees and science writer John Gribbin went so far as to say, 'There is no better evidence to support the argument that the universe has been designed for our benefit – tailor-made for man.' This particular fact made such an impact on the British astronomer Sir Fred Hoyle (the person who coined the term 'Big Bang') that he confessed, 'Nothing has shaken my atheism as much as this discovery.'

Pulling all of this together, there is compelling evidence that intelligent life on earth demands the unique arrangement of stars, planets and galaxies that is in fact in place. If the universe came into existence by chance or accident, there can be no rhyme or reason to it and no plan or purpose in it. Yet if there is no meaning in the existence of the universe, how can there be any meaning in life of any kind, let alone human life on our planet? As C. S. Lewis put it, 'Either there is significance in the whole process of things as well as in human activity, or there is no significance in human activity itself... You cannot have it both ways. If the world is meaningless, then so are we.' This all flags up a massive, fundamental question: what explains the existence of life? Peter Atkins' 'elaborate re-arrangement of nothing' hardly answers the question, nor can any other idea that atheism has to offer for the intricate fine-tuning in the universe, which needs to be precisely as it is to enable and sustain life. A straightforward illustration will help us to get the picture.

At the time of writing the tallest building in the United Kingdom is The Shard, the ninety-five storey skyscraper towering 309.6 metres over the streets of London. The largest piles underneath the building go down over 51 metres. The basement slab required the United Kingdom's largest-ever continuous pour; three concrete pumps emptied 700 truckloads over thirty-six hours. The completed building has over 111,480 square metres of floor space, 11,000 panes of glass and 305 flights of stairs. It houses a 200-bed 5-star hotel, seventy-two floors of high quality office space, three floors of restaurants and ten luxurious residences. The steel and glass spire at the top of The Shard includes 530 tons of structural steel.

Now for the illustration. If just one of the many thousands of screws used in building The Shard was not tightened correctly, do you think that the building would have collapsed and been rendered unusable? Then think of this: if the rate of expansion of the universe one second after it came into existence had been smaller by even one part in a hundred thousand million million it would have collapsed and we would not be here to discuss what had happened. The British physicist Paul Davies says that the balance between the effect of expansion and contraction was so precise that getting it right would be like aiming at a target an inch wide on the other side of the observable universe and hitting the mark. Every scientific discipline we know confirms that there is a reason for things being as they are. To say that this is true about everything except life itself is eccentric at best.

The American astronomer Allan Sandage, one of the fathers of modern astronomy, (and who discovered the first quasar) had no doubts about the matter: 'The world is too complicated in all its parts and interconnections to be due to chance alone. I am convinced that the existence of life with all its order in each of its organisms is simply too well put together.'

Over the last 200 years one idea has persuaded many people that the origin of life on our planet is found in the British biologist Charles Darwin's teaching on evolution. While not all evolutionists are atheists (we have no space here to go into that) all atheists are evolutionists, and Richard Dawkins even goes so far as to claim, 'It is absolutely safe to say that if you meet somebody who claims not to believe in evolution, that person is ignorant, stupid or insane.'

In his landmark book *The Origin of Species*, Darwin used 'The Tree of Life' as a metaphor to link all the world's organisms together and to claim that none was ever deliberately designed or created. Instead, he claimed that different forms of life gradually developed new characteristics, and when these became permanent a new species of family emerged, leading eventually to the human race.

Yet the 'tree of life' idea runs into deep trouble as soon as we examine its roots, as there is no explanation of the tree's existence. Darwin fantasized as to whether there might have been some 'warm little pond' with various chemicals floating around, and that a protein compound might somehow have been formed which could lead to more complex changes. Yet scientists have conducted countless experiments without being able to replicate this. As the American law professor and Intelligent Design leader Phillip Johnson puts it, 'There is no reason to believe that life has a tendency to emerge when the right chemicals are sloshing about in a soup... scientists employing the full power of their intelligence cannot manufacture living organisms from amino acids, sugars, and the like. *How then was the trick done before scientific intelligence was in existence?*' (To which we could add, 'And by whom?') The American biochemist Michael Behe gives us this picture: 'The probability of linking together just one hundred amino acids to create one protein molecule by chance would be the same as a blindfolded man finding one marked grain of sand somewhere in the vastness of the Sahara Desert – and doing it not just once, but three different times.' This explains why the Scottish anthropologist Sir Arthur Keith, who wrote the Foreword to the 100th edition of *Origin of Species*, admitted, 'Evolution is unproved and unprovable.'

As we will see in the second part of this book, the evolutionary theory ignores one of the most astonishing discoveries of recent years - the amazing properties of DNA (more about this later) – which are impossible to smuggle into a scenario that relies heavily on chance.

Does it make sense to sign up to atheism's claim that the finely tuned universe which allows life to flourish on earth is the result of an accidental rearrangement of nothing? Is it sensible to say that complex, intelligent life on our planet, with the built-in properties of DNA, has no firmer basis than the accidental shuffling of chemicals in some kind of global soup millions of years ago?

5 Does atheism make human sense?

Of the 8.7 million species on our planet, the human race is so distinct from all the others that it can be singled out and put under the microscope on its own to see whether atheism can explain its existence and characteristics. The top branches of Darwin's 'tree of life' are said to show that there is a close link between ape-like mammals and the human race. A long-running cartoon is based on this and shows two monkeys sitting in a cage. One asks the other, 'Am I my keeper's brother?' (a neat twist on words taken from an incident in the Bible.) We have all seen graphics showing 'ape-men' with barrel chests, jutting jaws and hairy legs, said to have emerged from earlier mammals and gradually developed a more erect posture until they walked upright. Yet these eye-catching graphics are a combination of guesswork and artwork, not a record of what actually happened.

A modern approach says that as human beings and chimpanzees have well over 95% of the same DNA they must be closely related, but this theory is torpedoed by the fact that DNA similarities have also been found among species which never suggest a link with humans. There is considerable DNA matching between human beings and cats, cows and fruit flies (to say nothing of about 50% between human beings and bananas). Similarity is not the same as relationship; no half man/half ape has ever been discovered, and a human being could not survive a blood transfusion from a chimpanzee.

Many of the species evolutionists say are 'lower down' the tree of life have superior features to humans. The common housefly's eyes can move ten times faster than a human's, the dolphin's hearing is much more acute, and a dog's sense of smell to a human's is what a symphony orchestra is to a tin whistle. The African elephant-snout fish has a brain weighing a lot more than a human's in relation to body weight, and some monkeys have brains twice as large as ours.

Yet when we take a closer look at a human being we are in a different world. The human frame is an engineering marvel largely made up of water and proteins, the rest being salts, lipids (mainly fats), carbohydrates and the two nucleic acids, DNA and RNA. A human body has about forty trillion cells, of more than 100 different types, and according to the American chemist, biochemist and educator Linus Pauling a single cell is 'more complex than New York City'. These cells, which specifically relate to different parts of the body, know exactly what to do because of the proteins they produce, and they produce proteins because of their DNA sequence. Yet as all these cells contain exactly the same DNA, why and how do they interpret the DNA information differently in order to do the right thing at the right time and in the right place if they were not created for a specific purpose?

Richard Dawkins admits that the human body gives the appearance of having been designed for a purpose; he says that it is 'supremely well designed, beautifully designed and far more complicated than any man-made machine.' He claims that 'the blind forces of physics could, given enough time, build these highly complicated machines' but admits that this process would need 'some luck to get started'. In the absence of any evidence that such a thing ever happened he invents a word — 'designoid' — to describe objects that he claims are not really designed, so can have no intended purpose. This is hardly good science, and guesswork is no substitute for truth.

The American physician, etymologist and educator Lewis Thomas saw things very differently. He was so amazed at what he discovered in the course of his research on the information-packed human gene that he said this: 'You start out as a single cell derived from the coupling of a sperm and egg; this divides into two, then four, then eight, and so on, and at a certain stage there emerges a single cell which will have as all its progeny the human brain…The mere existence of that cell should be one of the great astonishments of the earth. People ought to be walking around all day, all through their waking hours, calling to each other in endless wonderment, talking of nothing except that cell.' He then made this offer: 'If anyone does succeed in explaining it within my lifetime I will charter a skywriting airplane, maybe a whole fleet of them, and send them aloft to write one great exclamation point after another, around the whole sky, until my money runs out.' His funds were still intact when he died.

Stephen Hawking's claim that we are 'mere accumulations of fundamental particles' is clearly nonsense, and we have many other features that atheism is unable to explain. Consciousness is one. Richard Dawkins calls it 'the most profound mystery facing modern biology' and admits that 'we don't yet really have any idea how it evolved and where it fits into a Darwinian view of biology.' Yet we are not only conscious but self-conscious, constantly wanting to know who we are and our place in the universe. We ask 'Why?' and not just 'What?' We think about meaning and purpose. We want to know things, simply for the sake of knowing. We seek truth for its own sake. We long for significance. We reflect on the past, assess the present and speculate about the future.

Why do we do this? Atheism leans on the idea that given enough time these characteristics could gradually have developed from physical matter, but this is a laughable idea. Let me give a simple example. As I write this book I am sitting at a worktop designed to fit into the limited space available in my study. It is perfect for my needs and has served me ideally for years. Is it possible that given a vast amount of time (let us say a trillion years for starters) it could gradually become conscious, aware of its identity and of its particular place in the scheme of things? Would it ever reach the stage when it could think, hold opinions, make suggestions, reflect on people's ideas or respond to their actions? Would the time ever come when it could be jealous that another worktop was bigger or better?

If not, how did we make the leap from matter to mind? It makes no sense to argue that human consciousness and self-consciousness can evolve from something that is incapable of either. It is absurd to claim that thought has a material or physical basis. Jerry Fodor, the American philosopher and cognitive scientist concedes, 'Nobody has the slightest idea how anything material can be conscious.' Harvard University's Canadian-born cognitive scientist Steve Pinker, who was named Humanist of the Year in 2006, confirmed this when looking for an explanation of subjective consciousness: 'Beats the heck out of me. I have some prejudices, but no idea of how to begin to look for a defensible answer. And neither does anyone else.'

One particular spin-off from human self-consciousness is the in-built conviction that as human beings we have a unique sense of dignity that sets us apart from all other species. At a Prayer for America rally held in Yankee Stadium, New York on 23 September 2001, twelve days after the 9/11 terrorist attack, the actor James Earl Jones spoke for us all when he declared, 'We reaffirm our faith in the essential dignity of every individual.' So did US President Barack Obama, when at a ceremony in France in 2014 to mark the 70th anniversary of the 1944 D-Day invasion of Europe that turned the Second World War in the Allies' favour, he spoke of 'our commitment to... the inherent dignity of every human being.'

The British author Andrew Knowles put it neatly: 'I am a mystery. I wake up in the morning. I find myself the sole occupant of a complex, sensitive and extremely useful body. I am also the proud owner of an intricate, imaginative and highly resourceful brain. Everything about me is unique: my face, my fingerprints, my "self". I am alive. I develop. I grow. So does a vegetable. But I am more than a vegetable. Vegetables don't fall in love, or read the paper, or go on holiday... I am a body with a brain; an animal. But — I am more than an animal. Animals don't peer through telescopes, or send birthday cards, or play chess, or cook.'

Our sense of dignity is so ingrained that it extends even to the human body after death. The last English king to die in battle was Richard III, who was killed at the Battle of Bosworth Field in 1485. His body was buried in a crude grave in Greyfriars Friary, in Leicester, but its exact location was lost when the friary was demolished. Over 500 years later his remains were found under a car park. In the course of a furious row over where they should be reinterred, the Leader of Leicester City Council said, 'He deserves to be buried with dignity and honour in Leicester Cathedral' – and on 26 March 2015, the remains of England's last medieval king were finally laid to rest there. In 2014 the Paralympian athlete Oscar Pistorius stood trial in South Africa for the murder of his girlfriend Reeva Steenkamp. When Gert Saayman, the pathologist who carried out the post-mortem examination on the victim, went to the witness stand he asked that because of the graphic nature of the evidence he was about to give all live broadcasts of the trial be switched off to protect 'the dignity of the deceased'. Judge Thokozile Masipa agreed.

There are many other features that set man apart from every other species on our planet. To mention just one more, we have an aesthetic dimension; we make judgements about form, texture, colour, order and design, and are endlessly creative in developing new ways of expressing these. We compose and enjoy art, music and literature. We can appreciate beauty in things we see, hear, smell, touch and taste. Can atheism explain any of this? Richard Dawkins maintains, 'It is the plain truth that we are cousins of chimpanzees, somewhat more distant cousins of monkeys, more distant cousins still of aardvarks and manatees, yet more distant cousins of bananas and turnips.' His fellow atheist, the American biologist Jerry Coyne, says that 'the same forces that gave rise to ferns, mushrooms, lizards and squirrels also produced us,' while Christopher Hitchens claimed that we evolved 'from sightless bacteria.'

Does it make sense to believe any of them?

6 Does atheism make moral sense?

No right-minded person can deny that as human beings we have a moral dimension. Individuals may disagree as to whether a particular attitude or action is right or wrong, good or bad, but to make a judgement one way or the other points to some kind of moral law that seems to be programmed into our human software. As C. S. Lewis put it, 'Human beings, all over the earth, have this curious idea that they ought to behave in a certain way, and cannot get rid of it.' People may disagree on how the moral law applies in a given situation, but each one of us draws the line somewhere. In 2002 a man in Yorkshire was gouged to death with a screwdriver when he tried to stop thieves stealing a friend's car. Almost the first thing the police did was to appeal to professional car thieves to turn him in. They were banking on the fact that while these criminals had no scruples about stealing cars they drew the line at murder. In 2016 a man sentenced in the UK to twenty-two concurrent life sentences for raping or abusing 200 babies and young children was separated from other prison inmates for his own protection

A person does not have to believe in God or be in any way religious to have a moral dimension – we all have one; faith or lack of faith has nothing to do with it. Like it or not, we are moral creatures, with an inherent sense of right and wrong. The eighteenth-century German philosopher Immanuel Kant, a heavyweight thinker whose teaching influenced millions of people, said that two things filled his mind with 'ever new and increasing wonder and awe'; one was 'the starry heavens above' and the other 'the moral law within'. The question we need to ask is whether atheism has an explanation for this inner law that sets us apart from every other species on the planet. Does atheism help us to determine whether anything is morally right or wrong? Are we better equipped to make moral judgements without bringing God into the frame? Just as it is impossible to measure temperature without an absolute scale of reference, so it is impossible for us to distinguish the difference between right and wrong without an objective, independent reference against which to measure the difference. Does atheism have one?

It is one thing to say that there are no absolute moral standards, but to live as if none existed is another matter. Nobody goes through life as if morality was not an issue. The sense of right and wrong is so deeply embedded in us that we are instinctively affected by it. If somebody mistreats us, our normal reaction immediately shows that we believe in a moral standard that applies to both of us. When our conscience tells us that we ought (or ought not) to do something, does atheism give it any basis for telling us to go ahead – or to hold back? Wherever we stand on moral issues, we often distinguish between good and bad, better and worse, but how can we do this if there is no objective benchmark to guide us? Where can we find an independent basis for making these judgements? Atheism can give no coherent reason, but comes up with three theories.

The first is that morality is built into nature, of which the human species is part. This idea has a lot of supporters, but it collapses when it is cornered. In the first place it has to explain how such a dynamic reality first came into existence. As we saw earlier in this book, there is no known way in which life can independently spring out of non-life, and the 'morality in nature' idea faces a similar problem. If (as atheism says) the universe is nothing more than a cocktail of matter, energy, time and chance, when, how (and why) did morality come into the picture? How did atoms develop ethics? What is the link between molecules and morality? If things such as truth, justice, kindness and goodness are accidental ingredients of an impersonal universe, why do we attach such importance to them? How can anything in nature help us to define the words 'right' and 'wrong'? As the American historian and philosopher Herbert Schlossberg points out, 'Animals do not act morally or immorally; they only act naturally. A system of ethics that says human beings ought to base their behaviour on nature therefore justifies any behaviour, because *nature knows no ethic.*' Richard Dawkins agrees: 'The universe has no mind, no feelings and no personality... the universe doesn't care what people prefer.'

This is a massive problem for atheism, and relying on evolution to produce morality is another lost cause, as nobody has the slightest idea how it could do this. If our species is the by-product of millions of years of blind, purposeless forces, we are in the same boat as dandelions and dogs, cabbages and caterpillars. The American historian of science William Provine was a convinced atheist, but he openly admitted, 'Evolution teaches us virtually nothing about morality... We humans are just on our own. We're put here by a process that doesn't care about us, and we have to figure out for ourselves how to behave with each other.'

Richard Dawkins takes things even further: 'The universe we observe has precisely the properties we should expect if there is, at bottom, no design, no purpose, no evil and no good, nothing but blind, pitiless indifference... DNA neither cares nor knows. DNA just is. And we dance to its music.' But if this is the case, how can we condemn or punish law breakers of any kind if they too are simply driven by their DNA? When I was speaking at a meeting in Oxford an atheist shouted at me, 'Morality is relative', yet less than twenty-four hours earlier a Korean student at Virginia Polytechnic Institute and State University had killed thirty-two people and wounded seventeen others in the deadliest shooting incident by a single gunman in United States history. Was he merely dancing to the music of his genes? If so, how can we condemn him for what he did?

Turning the coin over, why do we honour, reward and admire those whose qualities lead them to act in ways that benefit countless other people if they too are doing no more than dancing to their DNA? Human moral standards must be either accidental and meaningless, or have a meaningful source outside of nature. C. S. Lewis is right to say, 'If we are to make moral judgements ... then we must believe that the conscience is not a product of Nature. It can be valid only if it is an offshoot of some absolute moral wisdom, a moral wisdom which exists absolutely "on its own" and is not a product of non-moral, non-rational Nature.'

The second atheistic theory is that moral standards are a matter of personal opinion. Nobody has expressed this more clearly than the American author Ernest Hemingway: 'What is moral is what you feel good after, and what is immoral is what you feel bad after.' This idea was echoed by one of the characters in the cult American television show *Melrose Place*: 'What's right is what you feel,' but this statement has so many flaws that beginning to list them is easier than knowing when to stop. In the first place, if morality is a matter of personal choice it would lead to total chaos in society, as everybody would be at liberty to pursue their own ends, regardless of how doing so would affect other people. The American psychiatrist Armand Nicholi makes the point well: 'If you disagree with me, who is right? If we have no moral point of reference, what you think is no more right or wrong than what I think.'

The fact that people have different standards is not proof that there is no ultimate standard. In fact, it is exactly the opposite; it shows that they are all subject to one. If there is no absolute right or wrong, how can we be sure that anything is either?There is a huge difference between preferences and principles, and nobody whose daughter was raped, whose car was stolen, or who in some other way suffered as the result of someone else's behaviour would settle for the first. Secondly, it removes any basis for a legal system, as someone charged with an offence of any kind could claim that their opinion as to what was right or wrong had the same standing as anyone else's, including those who framed the laws they are accused of breaking. Can we fine people, or send them to prison, over differences in personal opinion? Thirdly, it sets a person free of any obligation to behave properly towards anybody else. This may sound liberating, but it misses the point that everybody else would have the same liberty. To put this directly, if somebody cheated you in a business deal, stole something from you, assaulted you, or (if you are happily married) ran away with your spouse, there would be no point in complaining, as the person concerned could brush you aside and claim that their moral values allowed them to do so. Fourthly, treating morality as a matter of personal choice puts it on a par with choosing a meal in a restaurant – a decision with no moral content. In a world without God, how can we say that a lie is morally different from murder? Fifthly, relying on personal choice to define morality wipes out issues such as duty and responsibility and has no place for words like 'ought' and 'ought not'. Is there no objective reason why we should be morally good unless it pays off in some way?

The third atheistic theory is that morality is determined by current culture. Yet going with society's flow crashes into a cascade of questions. Why should public opinion be any better than private opinion? When two cultures clash, which one should we choose? What happens when a culture changes its stance and moves the goalposts? And why do we honour those who rejected contemporary culture and at great personal cost triggered changes in society that continue to benefit millions?

Does it make sense to go along with any of these ideas? – or to settle for Bertrand Russell's opinion that 'Outside human desires there is no moral standard.'?

On the other hand...

So far, we have looked at clues to help us answer the question our title asks. In doing so, we have seen the picture atheism presents. We could have traced other clues, but to keep this book to its intended size we will focus on exactly the opposite theory - that God *does* exist.

To do this means having a completely different worldview. A worldview is what a person assumes and believes to be true *before* coming to an opinion about anything else. For example, atheism is undoubtedly a worldview; atheists come to opinions about the universe, nature, human life, morality and everything else on the assumption that God does not exist. They face the same questions as everyone else about these subjects, but before they begin to frame their answers they rule out any possibility that God exists; as a leading American atheist put it, 'We cannot allow a Divine foot in the door.'

In *The God Delusion*, Richard Dawkins gets to what he calls 'the central argument' of the book; if God created everything else, who created God? We can obviously ask that about the ancient Greek or Roman gods, or about the thousands of gods that litter religious history, and the answer would always be 'man did'. However, Dawkins' question is about the God of whom the Bible speaks, and in asking his question he misses the crucial fact that the Bible points us to 'the eternal God' (Deuteronomy 33:27) who is 'from everlasting to everlasting' (Psalm 106:48) and, unlike all other gods, is not part of the universe. Instead, he is infinite, transcendent, omnipotent, intelligent and self-existent, beyond all restrictions of time and space, *and uncreated.* Infinity is not something our finite minds can grasp, but claiming that this rules out an eternal God is ignorance masquerading as intelligence. The God of whom the Bible speaks was not caused, nor can he be controlled or killed.

The Bible claims that its teaching is 'breathed out by God' (2 Timothy 3:16) and is his personal message to the human race. It is in this book that we find what he wants us to know about himself, the universe, the human race – and the meaning of life. Whatever you believe or do not believe, I ask you to read on and to see what things look like to someone with a God-centred worldview.

7 God makes cosmic sense

Nobody was there to see the universe come into being, nor can we conduct any experiment that gets within light years of duplicating what took place. It would seem reasonable to say that our only way of knowing what happened would be if it had a creator who tells us — and in the Bible's opening words he does so: 'In the beginning, God created the heavens and the earth' (Genesis 1:1). There is no single word in Hebrew (the language in which the early part of the Bible was originally written) that matches our English word 'universe', but *hassamayin we'et ha'ares* (translated 'the heavens and the earth') tells us that God created everything that exists outside of himself. Elsewhere, the Bible underlines this by stating, 'By him all things were created, in heaven and on earth, visible and invisible, whether thrones or dominions or rulers or authorities—all things were created through him and for him' (Colossians 1:16). The words 'all things' mean that God created all reality (including time and space). For Richard Dawkins to tell a BBC radio audience that the idea of creation 'doesn't do justice to the grandeur of the truth,' collides head-on with the evidence.

The English evolutionary biologist Andrew Parker, selected by The Royal Institution in 2000 as one of the top eight in the nation to be a 'Scientist for the New Century', is an atheist. Yet when he read what the Bible says about creation he came to this conclusion: 'Without expecting to find anything, I discovered a whole series of parallels between the creation story on the Bible's first page and the modern, scientific account of life's history... The more detail is examined, the more convincing and remarkable I believe the parallels become... The opening page of Genesis is scientifically accurate but was written long before the science was known. How did the writer of this page come to write this creation account...? I must admit, rather nervously as a scientist averse to entertaining such an idea, that the evidence that the writer of the opening page of the Bible was divinely inspired is strong. I have never before encountered such powerful, impartial evidence to suggest that the Bible is the product of divine inspiration.'

The Bible goes even further and puts the responsibility for believing what it says about God and creation firmly in our hands. It says that the universe reveals God's 'invisible attributes, namely his eternal power and divine nature', and that those who refuse to recognize this are 'without excuse.' (Romans 1:20). As the Welsh scientist Sir John Houghton, a winner of the Albert Einstein World Award for Science, puts it, 'The order and consistency we see in our science can be seen as reflecting orderliness and consistency in the character of God himself.' Does it take any more faith to believe this than to believe that the amazing order, harmony and beauty we see in the natural world is a gigantic fluke, that life itself sprang into existence by chance, that logic is sheer luck and that the vast amount of information in living things had no intelligent source? When we think of the vastness of the known universe it is impossible for us to grasp the amazing energy, skill and imagination needed to bring it into existence – but the Bible simply says, 'By the word of the LORD the heavens were made' - that 'he spoke, and it came to be' (Psalm 33:6,9). Yet the Welsh author Stuart Olyott is right to warn us, 'Nobody can plead that he is ignorant of the existence of God. It can clearly be seen that there is an Unseen.' In London's St Paul's Cathedral, the tomb of its architect, Sir Christopher Wren, has the Latin inscription, 'Reader: if you seek his monument, look around you.' The Bible says the same kind of thing: 'The heavens declare the glory of God, and the sky above proclaims his handiwork' (Psalm 19:1). The cosmos has no scientific reason for existing, yet we have seen in this book that the universal, elegant and consistent laws of nature are amazingly and precisely suited to allow life on our planet. There is no natural reason for this, and Keith Ward has no doubt that 'God is the best final explanation there can be for the universe.'

The American astronomer, physicist and cosmologist Robert Jastrow, the first Chairman of NASA's Lunar Exploration Committee, called himself 'an agnostic, and not a believer', yet in *God and the Astronomers* he wrote about the irony of trying to rule God out of the universe: 'For the scientist who has lived by his faith in the power of reason, the story ends like a bad dream. He has scaled the mountains of ignorance; he is about to conquer the highest peak; as he pulls himself over the final rock, he is greeted by a band of theologians who have been sitting there for centuries.'

8 God makes reasonable sense

Some years ago I was sitting alone in a coffee shop in the United States when I saw a strange-looking man wandering around as if he wanted someone to talk to. Without a book or newspaper with which to shield my face I just stared into my cup and hoped he would ignore me. No chance! He came over to my table and said, 'I'd like to ask you a question.' Thinking that I could probably reply with a quick one-liner and send him on his way, I replied, 'Go ahead.' Leaning over the table he looked me straight in the eye and asked, 'Where did thought come from?' Then before I could drum up a suitable reply he added, 'Now that makes you think, doesn't it?' – and with that he turned away and was gone.

I have never forgotten the incident, and have told the story countless times in lectures and other presentations, as the origin of thought is an issue that every atheist needs to face. Atheism says that a man's personality, hopes, aspirations and ideals are merely biological functions, and that human experiences such as knowing, imagining, feeling, loving and enjoying are nothing more than chemical reactions triggered off by physical movements in the brain. We have already exposed the folly of this kind of thinking and showed that it robs our thoughts of any moral, ethical or spiritual value.

C. S. Lewis underlined the point, and showed that if the human brain was never created for the purpose of coming to any rational conclusions, atheism is shunted into a dead-end: 'It is merely that when the atoms inside of my skull happen for physical or chemical reasons to arrange themselves in a certain way this gives me, as a by-product, the sensation I call thought. But if so, how can I trust my own thinking to be true? And if I can't trust my own thinking, I can't trust the argument leading to atheism, and therefore I have no reason to be an atheist. Unless I believe in God, I can't believe in thought, so *I can never use thought to disbelieve in God.*'

One way of checking whether God makes reasonable sense is to focus on the subject of logic, because without it reasonable thinking never gets off the ground. Without the laws of logic, we could never think sensibly about anything, let alone God's existence. The three most important laws of logic are The Law of Identity, The Law of Non-contradiction, and The Law of the Excluded Middle – and they are easily explained. Firstly, a thing is what it is: for example, a lorry is a lorry. Secondly, it cannot be something it is not: a lorry cannot be a tree at the same time. Thirdly, a statement is either true or false: there is no middle ground. These three laws are not matters of opinion, they are objective and undeniable. We never invented them, and they would exist whether or not we recognized or understood them. What is more, they are not physical or material, nor are they limited by location, culture or time.

This means that the laws of logic must have a transcendent and eternal source, a mind of which they are a reflection - and the Bible's very first words tick all these boxes: 'In the beginning, God created the heavens and the earth' (Genesis 1:1). This simple sentence fits all three of the fundamental laws of logic, and elsewhere the Bible underlines this when it says, 'In the beginning was the Word, and the Word was with God, and the Word was God' (John 1:1). The first six words of this quotation make it impossible to miss the connection with Genesis 1:1, and in the original language (Greek) 'Word' is *logos,* the word often used by Greek philosophers when speaking of the rational principle that governs the universe; it is also the root of our English word 'logic'. This points us to the fact that the laws of logic were not created by God; instead, they are a reflection of his nature, and of the way he thinks. It would not be an exaggeration to say that logic is one of his attributes. Logic is not God, yet the laws of logic can no more exist without him than your reflection in a mirror can exist without you.

The last paragraph embraces the very existence of the universe, but Stephen Hawking replaces Genesis 1:1 with this: 'Because there is a law of gravity, the universe can and will create itself out of nothing.' Yet this is not only self-contradictory - it says that the universe was created both by something (the law of gravity) yet by nothing - it gives no explanation for the fact that we have minds and can think about the subject. Nor does it help to say that first there was matter (the universe and all the stuff in it) and that some time later the human mind evolved. But when? And how? And why? C. S. Lewis shows where this idea leads: 'If minds are wholly dependent on brains, and brains on biochemistry and biochemistry (in the long run) on the meaningless flux of atoms, I cannot understand why the thought of those minds would have any more significance than the sound of wind in the trees.'

As atheism has no explanation for rationality, it can find no reason to claim that we are capable of thinking reasonably. Reasonable thinking is impossible without logic, and logic is not a material product. Instead, it demands a transcendent mind of which it is a true and dependable reflection. The Bible speaks of 'a God of knowledge' (1 Samuel 2:3), who is 'from everlasting to everlasting' (Psalm 90:2), whose understanding is 'beyond measure' (Psalm 147:5), and 'with whom there is no variation or shadow due to change' (James1:17).

This tells us that mind came before matter - the mind of God, who 'created all things' and by whose will 'they existed and were created' (Revelation 4:11). Included in the statement that God 'created man in his own image' (Genesis 1:27) is the fact that he has given us minds that enable us to make sense of the amazing universe in which he has placed us, and to discover and make use of the laws by which he governs it.

9 God makes scientific sense

There is no conflict between science and Christian faith –
and never has been. The conflict is between two worldviews,
one which rules God out and one which has God at its
centre. The first has faith in materialism, and says that the
explanation for the existence and nature of the universe lies
within itself. The second has faith in God. It says that
without his decision to create it the universe would not even
exist; God did not create because he had to, but because he
chose to.

The universally accepted First and Second Laws of
Thermodynamics are relevant here. The First Law says that
matter and energy can neither be self-created nor destroyed.
This means that the cosmos could not have brought itself
into existence. Yet there has to have been a moment when
energy, matter, time and space came into existence. If an
eternal, infinite, transcendent God is ruled out where can
the atheist turn to explain the origin of the cosmos? The
British physicist and engineer Edgar Andrews pinpoints the
problem, 'No matter how close to the instant of origin one
may be able to press the scientific model of the cosmos, it
remains impossible for such an explanation to be applied at

or before the time zero point. It therefore follows that science, even at its most speculative, must stop short of offering any explanation or even description of the actual event of origin.' The Second Law backs this up by teaching that matter in the cosmos is becoming increasingly disorganized as its energy is dissipated – and so points to a time in the past when it had a highly ordered beginning.

Scientists have done a brilliant job in discovering the laws that govern the universe. The laws of thermodynamics, the law of gravity, and many others, give us fascinating insights into what makes the universe 'tick', but to go beyond that and to claim with Stephen Hawking that 'multiple universes arise naturally from physical law' is to slide from fact to fantasy. Science can only make progress because the laws of physics are universally consistent, guaranteeing that the cosmos is orderly and predictable. Scientists therefore rely on laws *that are already there.* But who or what is the super intellect behind these laws? The laws of physics can create nothing, nor can they cause anything to happen. They help us to understand how the universe works, but tell us nothing about how it (or they) came into existence. To give one simple example, the law of gravity tells us that near our planet a freefalling object accelerates at the rate of 975.36 centimetres per second per second. Man discovered this formula, but he did not invent it, and the mathematical precision of the laws of physics convinced Einstein that we need to look beyond the universe to explain it: 'Everyone who is seriously engaged in the pursuit of science becomes convinced that the laws of nature manifest the existence of a spirit vastly superior to that of men, and one in the face of which we with our modest powers must feel humble.' Science gives us powerful reasons for such faith.

The Bible endorses these and says that Einstein's 'vastly superior' spirit is God, who 'upholds the universe by the word of his power' (Hebrews 1:3). Elsewhere, we are told not only that 'all things were created through him and for him,' but that 'he is before all things, and in him all things hold together' (Colossians 1:16-17). God's transcendent wisdom and power formulated the laws of physics that explain why we have a cosmos, not chaos. John Lennox testifies, 'The beauty of the scientific laws reinforces my faith in an intelligent, divine Creator.'

A God-centred worldview makes perfect sense of the elegance, balance and beauty of the laws governing the universe. The order, discipline and consistency we see in the elements that make life possible on our planet are what we should expect if they were brought into existence by a Creator whose own character is consistently perfect. One of the most outstanding scientists in history was James Joule. As well as the ground-breaking achievements we noted earlier, he made massive contributions to unifying the fragments of physics, was the first to calculate the velocity of gas molecules and was one of the first to recognize the need for standard units of electricity. He also demonstrated the validity of the principle of energy conservation, which formed the basis of the First Law of Thermodynamics, which has been called 'one of the most important generalizations in the history of science'. Joule was convinced that one of man's greatest aims should be 'to know something of (God's) attributes of wisdom, power and goodness as evidenced by his handiwork' and that 'an acquaintance with natural laws means no less than an acquaintance with the mind of God therein expressed.'

A God-centred worldview reveals truth that goes far beyond that of its opposite. It sees God not only as the Creator and sustainer of the universe, but as the one who sets out the purposes for which it was made and who establishes its values and meaning. The Bible tells us, 'Set your minds on things that are above, not on things that are on earth' (Colossians 3:2). It also gives us the best possible motive: 'For the things that are seen are transient, but the things that are unseen are eternal' (2 Corinthians 4:18).

10 God makes living sense

In its article on 'Life', *Encyclopedia Britannica* claims, 'A great deal is known about life,' then goes on to say that 'despite the enormous fund of information' scientists have discovered, 'it is a remarkable fact that no general agreement exists on what it is that is being studied. *There is no generally accepted definition of life.*' Yet we all recognize the difference between life and non-life; life is something we find in strawberries but not in steel, in donkeys but not in diamonds, in people but not in plastic. The qualities, properties, characteristics and implications of what we call 'life' are so important that we should surely want to know where it came from?

One day in 1953, the British molecular biologist Francis Crick breezed into his local pub in Cambridge and announced, 'We've found the secret of life.' This was more than a little over the top, but perfectly understandable, as he and his colleague James Watson had just discovered the exact structure of deoxyribonucleic acid (universally known as DNA). A DNA molecule consists of two sugar-phosphate strands coiled around each other to form a double helix, and it was this discovery that got Crick and Watson so excited. DNA carries all the genetic instructions that determine the growth, development, function and reproduction of all known living organisms, and of many viruses. It is what triggers into action all the features a living organism needs to live and grow. Without it, the amino-acids a living being needs would be lying around like unused bricks on a building site.

DNA is crammed with so much information that it is a miniature marvel, unequalled by anything in the most advanced modern technology. For example, the data needed to specify the design of a human being, including physical characteristics such as hair, skin, eyes and height, and determining the arrangement of components including over 200 bones, 600 muscles, over 110,000,000 nerve fibres, 100 billion nerve cells and 400 billion feet of blood vessels and capillaries, are packed into a unit several thousand million million times smaller than the smallest piece of functional machinery ever used by man, and weighing less than a few thousand-millionths of a gram. It has been estimated that on the same scale all the information needed to specify the design of the hundreds of millions of species that have ever existed on our planet could be held in a teaspoon, and there would still be room left over for all the information contained in every book ever written. Another estimate says that it would take a stack of books that would encircle our planet 5,000 times to contain the information in a mere pinhead of DNA.

Each one of the trillions of cells in the human body contains exactly the same DNA, yet these cells do different things. The English geneticist Alison Woollard told listeners to the BBC Radio 4 programme *Start the Week,* 'We know that cells know what to do because of the proteins they produce, and that they produce proteins because of the DNA sequence that they have inside all of our cells... So how is it that cells can interpret this information in different ways, in order for cells to do the right thing at the right time and in the right place?' She offered no answer to the question, but Francis Collins has no doubt as to where the evidence points: 'The God of the Bible is also the God of the genome. He can be worshipped in the cathedral or in the laboratory. His creation is majestic, awesome, intricate and beautiful.'

C. Everett Koop, widely regarded as the most influential Surgeon General in American history, had no hesitation in adding this testimony: 'If I didn't believe that I had a God who was solid and dependable, a God who makes no mistakes, I couldn't continue what I'm doing. I never operate without having a sub-conscious feeling that there's no way this extraordinarily complicated mechanism known as the human body just happened to come up from slime and ooze... When I make an incision with my scalpel, I see organs of such intricacy that there simply hasn't been enough time for natural evolutionary processes to have developed them.'

Collins and Koop are saying that God makes living sense, that he (and he alone) is the explanation for all life, wherever we find it. We have already seen that Richard Dawkins admits 'living things are not only designed, they are supremely well designed, beautifully designed and far more complicated than any man-made machine' but then he makes the jaw-dropping claim that, given enough time, living things could be built by 'the blind forces of physics'. This takes God out of the frame - but it does the same thing to common sense.

Reflecting on the discovery of new genes, Francis Collins says, 'There is a sense in which those moments of discovery also become moments of worship, moments of appreciation, of the incredible intricacies and beauty of biology, of the world, of life - and therefore an appreciation of God as the Creator.'

The Bible speaks of God's 'eternal power' (Romans 1:20), and 'the immeasurable greatness of his power' (Ephesians 1:19). It says that he 'does great things and unsearchable, marvellous things without number' (Job 5:9). Time and again he is called 'the Lord Almighty' (e.g. 2 Corinthians 6:18). This tells us that he can do whatever he chooses to do whenever he chooses to do it and for whatever purpose he has in mind. We can take this right back to the creation of the universe and everything in it; the Bible specifically says of him that 'you created all things, and by your will they existed and were created' (Revelation 4:11).

Part of the Bible's creation narrative fills out the 'all things'. It tells us of the point at which God created 'every living creature that moves' (Genesis 1:21). This is the first specific mention in the narrative of the source of life, though before this the earth 'brought forth vegetation' (Genesis 1:12) at God's command, every species capable of reproducing 'according to their own kinds' (Genesis 1:12). Later, we are told that when God created the first human being he 'breathed into his nostrils the breath of life, and the man became a living creature' (Genesis 2:7). Centuries later, one of the Bible's authors acknowledged to God, 'For you formed my inward parts; you knitted me together in my mother's womb. I praise you, for I am fearfully and wonderfully made. Wonderful are your works; my soul knows it very well' (Psalm 139:13-14).

11 God makes human sense

The English social anthropologist Edmund Leach claimed, 'There is no sharp break between what is human and what is mechanical,' and the Polish-born British mathematician and biologist Jacob Bronowski once assured us that man 'is not different in kind from any other forms of life', that 'living matter is not different in kind from dead matter', and that 'man is part of nature, in the same sense that a stone is, or a cactus, or a camel'. Yet the fact that these men could think and say such things proves that they were wrong, as nothing that is 'mechanical' or 'dead matter' is able to discuss whether it is related to anything else. There is a massive difference not only between life and non-life but between human beings and all other living creatures, even though a human being has fewer chromosomes than (for example) an agrodiaetus butterfly, an African hedgehog, a wolf or a donkey. The issue is so important that we need to drill a little deeper into this, and a God-centred worldview helps us to do this.

C. S. Lewis pointed out, 'One of the things that distinguishes man from the other animals is that he wants to know things, wants to find out what reality is like, simply for the sake of knowing.' This is a very different assessment than that by Peter Atkins, who writes the human race off as 'a bit of slime on a planet'. It also conflicts with Richard Dawkins' insistence that we are nothing more than survival machines – 'robot vehicles blindly programmed to preserve the selfish molecules known as genes.'

Most of us find it difficult if not impossible to buy into this bleak scenario, and we find ourselves wanting to look for a deeper meaning to life. In the previous section we have looked at humankind's remarkable physical features, but we now need to dig deeper and ask whether there is an explanation for other remarkable features which show us to be unique, marking us out from every other living being on our planet. Why do we have personality? Why are we capable of intelligent thinking? Why do we use propositional language (language that joins propositions together to produce more complex language)? Why do we have an aesthetic dimension and are so creative in wood, stone, metal and other materials, as well as in the worlds of music, painting and literature? Above all why do we have a spiritual dimension? As we look for answers to these questions, an atheist worldview gives us no clue. On the other hand, a God-centred worldview looks to a single statement in the Bible that points us towards the clear answer to them all: 'So God created man in his own image, in the image of God he created him; male and female he created them' (Genesis 1:27).

The Bible does not explain what this means, but before we see why it answers the last paragraph's questions, we need to be clear what this statement is *not* saying. It is not saying that man was created in the same size, shape or weight as God. 'God is spirit' (John 4:24) and as such has no physical features or material properties, and no parts or dimensions. Everything God created originally reflected something of his own character, but only man was created 'in the image of God', a description that includes his knowledge of his Maker, his intimate relationship to him, and his authority to rule over our planet. When the creation of the entire cosmos and everything in it was completed, 'God saw everything that he had made' and pronounced it 'very good' (Genesis 1:31). There was a time when perfect people, in a perfect relationship with God and with each other, lived in a perfect environment. The situation now is very different, but even in a broken world we can find evidence that a God-centred worldview answers the questions we are asking.

It tells us why we have personality. God is not mechanical or material, but personal. He is not cosmic dust, atmospheric energy or some vague 'higher power.' He thinks, chooses, cares, makes (and keeps) promises, and gives warnings and directions. Man's creation 'in the image of God' explains why we are persons and not, as someone has put it, 'computers made of meat'. The ultimate fact about the universe is a personal God who gives us personality.

It tells us why we are *homo sapiens,* capable of intelligent thinking. The Bible speaks of 'the depth of the riches and wisdom and knowledge of God' (Romans 11:33). It says that 'his understanding is unsearchable' (Isaiah 40:28) and that he is 'perfect in knowledge' (Job 37:16). To nail the point down, it states simply that 'he knows everything' (1 John 3:20). None of this knowledge has ever been acquired; God knows everything (past, present and future) because of who he is. Every shred of intelligence, information or insight we have as human beings is because man was made 'in the image of God', who granted him the intellectual capacity he needed to exercise dominion over the earth, and to live in a way that reflected the divine source of his knowledge. We can never know everything that God knows (which explains why there are times when we fail to understand why he allows certain thing to happen). Yet whenever we discover truth, in anything from astronomy to ethics, it is because in his wisdom God has allowed us to do. This is why Johannes Kepler, who discovered the three laws of planetary motion, said of his work that he was 'merely thinking God's thoughts after him'.

It tells us why we use propositional language. One of the clearest things the Bible says about God is that he speaks to us. One way in which he does so is by means of the material universe we see all around us. As we saw earlier, 'The heavens declare the glory of God, and the sky above proclaims his handiwork' (Psalm 19:1). The whole of nature is what someone has called 'an unlimited broadcasting system through which God speaks to us every hour, if only we will tune him in'. Whether we use a telescope or a microscope we should be struck by evidence of God's power, precision, inventiveness and imagination. He also speaks through the Bible, 'the living and abiding word of God' (1 Peter 1:23). As we have already seen, its claims can be summarized in the simple statement, 'All Scripture is breathed out by God' (2 Timothy 3:16). The Bible claims from cover to cover that it is God's direct, verbal message to man; no other publication comes close to doing this. In it, we read many times of people speaking directly to God, and of God responding to them (and vice versa). This alone should be enough to tell us that being made 'in the image of God' enables us to use language in the way that we do.

It tells us why we have an aesthetic dimension and are so endlessly creative. The Bible speaks of 'the beauty of the LORD' (Psalm 27:4), a phrase that summarizes the perfection of all the qualities by which he is 'clothed with splendour and majesty' (Psalm 104:1). Nature is an amazing exhibition of God's beauty, and of his creative skill and ingenuity. The Bible says, 'He made everything beautiful in its time' (Ecclesiastes 3:11) and in its original perfection pronounced it 'very good'. Our human appreciation of beauty, and our ability to create it, reflect our Maker's beauty and creativity.

It tells us why we have a spiritual dimension. Being made 'in the image of God' explains why only God can meet our innermost needs. Man was not only made *by* God, but *for* God, who gave him the capacity to enjoy a living relationship with him. God 'has put eternity into man's heart' (Ecclesiastes 3:11) and only he can fill what has been called the 'God-shaped gap' in human lives.

12 God makes moral sense

As we saw much earlier, human beings all have a moral dimension, a built-in sense that there is a difference between right and wrong. Richard Dawkins is right to say, 'We are all, to a greater or lesser extent, moral,' but he then confesses, 'I haven't a very well worked-out story of where that comes from.' This is not surprising, as the theory of evolution can produce no basis for it. As Dawkins admits, 'Much as we may wish to believe otherwise, universal love and the welfare of the species as a whole are concepts which simply do not make evolutionary sense.'

The words 'good', 'better', 'bad' and 'worse' all assume that they have some kind of moral framework. Ideas of morality differ from person to person and from one society to another, but none of them makes solid sense without such a framework. The British philosopher C. Stephen Evans hit the nail on the head here: 'It is right to be kind, generous, honest, courageous and just. It is wrong to be selfish, cruel, deceptive and cowardly. It is wrong to be abusive, unfriendly and ungrateful. These are truths which human beings discover. We do not invent them; in their own way they are as objective as the laws of science or mathematics.'

The fact is that we usually call something morally wrong only by contrasting it with what we believe to be morally right – but unless there is an objective moral law our judgement can never be more reliable than personal opinion, which can change at the drop of a hat. Where can we find a solid basis on which to build a secure point of reference for making moral judgements? The British philosopher Peter S. Williams tells us where to look: 'The most plausible explanation of the existence of objective moral values, and our knowledge (however imperfect) of these values... is that there exists an all-good, personal, rational and eternal being who has made humans in his image.'

A God-centred worldview provides us with this picture. It reveals that our moral sense comes from our Creator, whose perfection is the absolute standard by which all our instincts and ideas are to be measured. As the British author John Benton says, 'God's own character is the fundamental basis for what is right and just. He is the holy God who is the foundation of all creation. His character is what is right and good, and all that offends against the holy character of God is therefore wrong, and wrong in the most absolute sense.' This means that God's commands are good because God is not only perfectly good, but the perfect source of all goodness.

Other animals are driven solely by instinct, but as human beings we have a conscience, a moral monitor that distinguishes between right and wrong, tells us which to choose, and passes independent judgement on our behaviour. There are times when conscience prompts us to be generous to people we are never likely to meet, and from whom we can expect no benefit in return. Do we see this anywhere else in nature? The English theologian Rod Garner makes the same point with a humorous slant: 'Rats, after all, as far as we know, show no particular enthusiasm for moral issues and questions of meaning; and chimpanzees, delightful though they are, are not normally to be seen on our streets collecting money for impoverished chimpanzees they will never meet.' Our in-built moral monitor is not fundamentally based on our culture, upbringing or education. Instead, it is God's fingerprint on the human psyche, pointing us (even if we fail to recognize it) to the fact that we are all subject to his moral law, regardless of whether or not we believe that he exists. God alone gives human life its ultimate moral reference point. As the Russian novelist and historian Aleksandr Solzhenitsyn put it, 'The line between good and evil passes not through states, nor between classes, nor between political classes either, but right through the middle of every human heart and through all human hearts.'

Even those who have never heard of God have his law 'written on their hearts' (Romans 2:15). As we saw earlier, this is the 'moral law within' that filled Immanuel Kant's mind with 'increasing wonder and awe'. A God-centred worldview not only explains why this law exists, but why we instinctively act on it. The conscience can be stifled and suppressed, but in Paul Johnson's phrase, 'It is made of psychic indiarubber and springs back, however unwanted or unheeded, to wag a finger at us.'

Conscience kicks in whenever we deliberately violate whatever we think is right - which is more often than we care to admit. If we deny that we ever do this, 'we deceive ourselves, and the truth is not in us' (1 John 1:8). We are all exposed to God's law in one way or another – *and exposed by it as lawbreakers*. Nobody even comes close to meeting its demands, as the Bible bluntly puts it when saying that 'all have sinned and fall short of the glory of God' (Romans 3:23). When it asks, 'Who can say, "I have made my heart pure; I am clean from my sin"?' (Proverbs 20:9) we all know the only honest answer to the question. But that is not the end of the matter. There are consequences...

13 The last word

Asked how she would like to be remembered after she died, the Australian journalist Germaine Greer replied, 'Compost. I'd want people to say, "She made good compost."' This ties in with atheism's creed, which says in effect that we begin as a fluke, live as a farce, and end as fertilizer. If this is true, death wipes out everything we think, say and do in this life, and means that the destinies of the worst and best of people are identical. We all end up (as one of my golfing contacts puts it) 'on the wrong side of the grass' – with nothing to follow. This echoes Bertrand Russell's opinion that 'when I die I shall rot, and nothing of my ego will survive.' The French philosopher Jean-Paul Sartre also settled for this when he wrote, 'Man is a useless passion. It is meaningless that we live and it is meaningless that we die.' Yet this flatly contradicts the Bible's teaching that man is not only 'appointed to die,' but 'after that comes judgement' (Hebrews 9:27). Trying to avoid God (either by denying that he exists or by refusing to have anything to do with him) is utterly pointless, as the day is coming when 'each one of us will give an account of himself to God' (Romans 14:12).

Every one of our thoughts, words and actions will then be exposed: 'For nothing is hidden that will not be made manifest, nor is anything secret that will not be known and come to light' (Luke 8:17). God 'will bring every deed into judgement, with every secret thing, whether good or evil' (Ecclesiastes 12:14), and as he is 'righteous in all his ways' (Psalm 145:17) his judgement will be flawless. On that day, 'God's righteous judgement will be revealed' (Romans 2:5) and as 'the LORD is a God of justice' (Isaiah 30:18), absolute, ultimate and perfect justice will be done, and will be seen to be done, with not a single case in which it will be too lenient or too severe. Atheists need to grasp this, as we live in a world when perfect justice is often no more than a pipe dream. All too often people get away with murder (literally and metaphorically), the good die young, the innocent suffer, cheats prosper and crime pays. The British philosopher John Stuart Mill, a passionate atheist, agreed that 'the order of things in this life is often an example of injustice, not justice'. But if there is no God, there will never be a day of final judgement, in which case none of this world's injustices will ever be overturned. This brings two massive factors into the picture.

The first is God's complete and infallible knowledge of us. Even as we go about our present lives, 'no creature is hidden from his sight, but all are naked and exposed to the eyes of him to whom we must give account' (Hebrews 4:13). The Bible goes into specifics about this, but one example is enough to make the point here: 'Whatever you have said in the dark shall be heard in the light, and what you have whispered in private rooms shall be proclaimed on the housetops' (Luke 12:3). Even things we have so carefully hidden from others will be revealed. Can anyone seriously shrug that off? None of us would like to share with other people *everything* we have thought, said or done, but on the day of judgement nothing will be hidden from God.

The second is that as far as heaven is concerned 'nothing unclean will ever enter it' (Revelation 21:27). God is a God of perfect holiness and has zero tolerance of everything that comes short of this. He is 'of purer eyes than to see evil' (Habakkuk 1:13), which is one of the Bible's ways of telling us about God's eternal home. This will be 'a new heaven and a new earth' (Revelation 21:1), a perfectly restored creation in which everyone there will enjoy a perfectly restored relationship with their Creator. Nothing that scars and stains life now will be present. There will be the complete absence of pain, doubt, anger, fear, sorrow, sadness, frustration and regret. There will be nothing to grieve over, no unanswered questions, no humiliating ignorance and no unsatisfied desires. Nor will there be sin of any kind. Nobody will have either the inclination or the ability to sin in any way; instead, everything they do will reflect the glory of God and fulfil the very purpose for which they were created.

This stupendous scenario raises a crucial question: how could such a thing be possible? The answer is that God himself has done something truly amazing to bring it about. 'God has landed on this enemy-occupied planet in human form' was C. S. Lewis' way of saying that about 2,000 years ago God himself, in the person of Jesus Christ, came into our world to rescue rebellious sinners and to bring them into a living relationship with himself, both in this life and in the life to come. God did not send a third party to rescue us; he came himself. In this way, 'the goodness and loving kindness of God our Saviour appeared' (Titus 3:4). Jesus was 'the radiance of the glory of God and the exact imprint of his nature' (Hebrews 1:3); in him, 'all the fullness of God was pleased to dwell' (Colossians 1:19).

Not only was Jesus born without sin, he lived a perfect life, meeting all the demands of God's holy law; the Bible specifically tells us that although he was 'tempted as we are' he was 'without sin' (Hebrews 4:15). Then, in the greatest act of love ever performed, and after being betrayed, reviled and tortured, he deliberately allowed himself to be put to death in the place of sinners, and in his own body and spirit paid the penalty sinners deserved. In the Bible's words, Jesus died, 'the righteous for the unrighteous, that he might bring us to God' (1 Peter 3:18). The clearest proof we have that in his death Jesus paid the full penalty for human sin is that within three days he rose from the dead, and now 'death no longer has dominion over him' (Romans 6:9). The overwhelming evidence for this has never been shaken, and as C. S. Lewis wrote, 'He has forced open a door that had been locked since the death of the first man. He has met, fought and beaten the King of Death. Everything is different because he has done so. This is the beginning of the new creation. A new chapter in cosmic history has opened.'

We have already seen that with our track record there is no way in which we can spend eternity in God's presence, but the reason why the core message of Christianity is called 'the gospel' (good news) is that in his life, death and resurrection Jesus has provided a way for us to do so. He did not come into the world to condemn us but to save us, and to all who put their trust in him (instead of hoping that they can somehow get right with God under their own steam) he makes the amazing promise that they immediately receive the forgiveness of sins and eternal life. For them there will be 'no condemnation' (Romans 8:1) on the day of final judgement because Jesus has already paid in full the punishment they deserved.

As every moment brings you closer to that inevitable day, does it make sense to hold on to a worldview that ignores God, rejects his loving offer of forgiveness and eternal life, and leads you to an appalling destiny in hell, paying forever the penalty your sins deserve?

Does atheism make sense?